To Mum, D
and J
and everyone who [...]
to make and share these poems

Front Cover image by Stanley Donwood:
"What we have here is some kind of hateful monster orchestrating a rain of incendiaries upon a burning city. Operation Phantom Fury was the codename given to the US military assault on the Iraqi city of Falluja in November 2004."

With massive thanks from the author for use of this image.

Stanley Donwood, amongst other creations, produces Radiohead's artwork. For more of his art, and his writing, go to *www.slowlydownward.com*

ISBN: 978-0-9566793-0-7

Published by James Oliver, Sheffield 2010

Copyfree: In the event that anyone would want to reprint/republish any of these poems, they are free to do so.

Contents

Restless and Rooted

Meadowhell	7
Gym Going	8
Poverty of Politics	10
The Melancholy of Airports	12
Moonscape	13
Trance Nation	14
Climb	16
Whitby, Jan 2007	18
Peace is a Park in Sheffield	19
A Specific Theory of Relativity	20

Think the Unthinkable

Think the Unthinkable	23
"Fuck Off"	26
International Currency Exchanges	28
Address to the People	30
Coping with Maggots	32
Epitaphs for Larkin	34
The Emperor's New Socialism	35
Paper Chase	36
Rumble in the Jungle	37

Smoulder and Spark

Red Carpet	41
Dropping Bombs and Food	42
War as Peace: Stage Management	44
The Hidden Fist	46
Satellite Links	47
Smoulder and Spark	48
Taste and Decency	50

Sculpture Poems

Yin Yang	55
Worter Macht Frei	56
Epilogue	57
Spirals	58
Untitled	59

Kashmir

Kashmir	63
Dust to Dust	64
For my Comrades in Bagh	65
Untitled, Bagh 2006	66

Epilogue

Escapology	69

Restless and Rooted

Meadowhall- Sheffield shopping centre built on the site of an old steel works

Meadowhell

we were once ejected from the temple
for inciting workers to join unions
redundantly
as most were too scared
to even take a leaflet

and at ground zero
two bronze steel workers
stand witness
to their own demise;
beaten into shape;
both colossal
and petrified

I recently read about a sociology study of gyms, which is summed up by this slightly sinister blurb:

"Beyond the body, the social world of the gym is important. The gym is a place to make and meet friends, a site of social interaction and a source of social capital."
In the Gym: Motives, Meaning and Moral Careers

The poem's persona is part Patrick Bateman from *American Psycho*. Unless you know different, this is the only satirical poem to sample Matthew Wilder's 80s pop classic A*int Nothing Gonna Break my Stride...*

Gym-Going

I'm working up a sweat
watching hip-hop-honeys
on the screen
and I can flirt from a cross-trainer
without breaking my stride

aint nothing gonna break
my stride
nobody gonna slow me down
I'm gym going

I've got an elite personal trainer
for the darkness in my soul
and I'm going to ab-attack
to get my core back

aint nothing gonna break
my stride
nobody gonna slow me down
I'm gym going

I'm hardening my pecs
to better protect my heart
and hide a multitude of sins

aint nothing gonna break
my stride
nobody gonna slow me down
I'm gym going

I'm asset stripping my corporate body
and I've got interpersonal interactions
down to 10 second bursts
I'm burning off my competitors like carbs

aint nothing gonna break
my stride
nobody gonna slow me down
I'm gym going

so why is it, when I'm scaling
the automatic wall
I feel I'm climbing
into, not out of
our own abyss?

aint nothing gonna break
our stride
nobody gonna slow us down
we're gym going

A Blairite spin on educational underachievement was to blame it on the 'poverty of aspiration' caused by left-wing teachers using poverty as an excuse

Poverty of Politics

crouched at the front of the class, a small, coiled frame,
lion-like hair and eyes, and a face guarded by freckles and ferocity
your spirit, like many, still haunts me
from a place I hardly reached

and like many, the class-list registered a change of surname
but nothing of the pressures that piled up to that seismic
shift, or the fallout

like the ones cut off by the electric, gas, or both
or like most of you
cut off by someone else's English

and at the slightest challenge you'd get mardy as hell
hackles up, eyes roaring, voice aflame
your indignance
a search for the root of that word
and though help was considered
counseling wasn't on the curriculum
and besides, it cost
and money fled the needs of this side of town
to elope with middle-class company
as fast as the dynamic New Labour Party
even the trains no longer served Rossington;
a pitless village, whose roads all now converged
on nothing

and though you once told me you only had concentration for footy
and bikes
we managed to cajole you one lesson
into a walk-on part in front of the video-camera
and outside yourself
in that costume-suit
you soon settled into a frame

where people laughed at you by your will
and the games within were not played on you
but by you;
you couldn't get enough

and when you looked through the viewfinder
to replay your moment of glory
you seemed spellbound
and I wondered
did you see in that reflection
any of the awkwardness or loss
that the camera inadvertently captured
in your movement constrained by script
or the trajectory
in the back of your eye
that the lens could only hint at
but that I saw you rehearse every day:

compact
hard-shined
mottled fury
hurled careless down a hired lane
the impotent skittles exploding
and the bars coming down
behind you

The Melancholy of Airports

all these people
urgently heading somewhere
seem struck by a surprising melancholy

as if these neon lights
moving walkways
luggage carousels
and endless lists
of destinations

only remind them
they have no idea
of where they want to be
or how to get there

I wrote this on hearing of one of the many internment camps in occupied Palestine, where young men are routinely rounded up and held without trial, where prisoners who asked for their location were dismissively told by the guards- "On the moon."

Moonscape

what do they dream in Palestine?
of a wall that slowly
spirals
in
coiling like a snake
till all dreams
are steel

and those taken from their earth
and interned in orbit
who ask not why they are taken
or when they will be released
but simply where they are
have been told that this other prison
is on the moon

and maybe they dream there
of thoughts open and weightless
of a landscape peaceful and silent
in which olive trees
and children
and water
      run forever

Trance Nation

Blood-rush brain-buzz eyes wide open skin-tingling
anticipation, lights turn us on in subterranean dark
carnivalesque costume and art retell us as friendly-strange
here to weave a ritual of anonymous intimacy

as a substance on the tongue transubstantiates
to guide the mass to shared spiritual states
so language also is soldered to ceremony:
Loved-up, Coming-up, Coming-down, Chilling-out
but the sound itself is the ephemeral script:

Beneath everything the womb-beat pumps
rhythm rushes to ride the heartbeats
Techno breaks into the House
and keyboards escalate to precarious heights
percussion accelerates the hungry heat
and a thousand hearts explode and recreate
as one wild pumping animal

Cut to the beatific frenetic riots of jungle
crushed in stairwells, staggering back and fighting on
with anger compressed each decade
in back rooms and tower blocks
from rock through reggae punk and rap
galvanised to this pile up of apocalyptic
high rise collisions clearing space for explosions
into epiphanies of wide undreamt-of space and freedom

Trance washes in, dusk-soaked,
receding in a glissando of cascading shells
swashing deep to the waving of stoned coral reefs
and fish drifting, stunned in each other's beauty

Water is vicarious worship; raised to the light
that illuminates, it becomes the essence of all our wild
unattainable dreams of purity. Inside us or held aloft
it is a prism, catching the light and scattering it
to the darkest corners of our yearning cells

passed from hand to hand, mouth to mouth,
we nod and smile like Buddhist monks,
unwitting spiritualists we illuminate
the depths of the instant
in the simplicities of our exchange

DJs are fiendish bodhisattvas
looping kills and rewinds, deaths and births
scratching a living out of discs of vinyl
delivering us to temptation:

our communal individualities that we perform amongst each other
and our individual communality, in the different ways
we hold each other together;
in this we must recognise the greatest blasphemy,
that all power is in ourselves, and together.
if not
then this remains a temple
which has no world

Climb
for John Kirkman, and those who remember him

always climbing, the time when you
slipped, and the other when you
plummeted, it took more than risk
and having more metal than bone in your ankles
to stop you gripping that rock again.
each blow fate dealt you was another overhang,
the next grade to conquer

and you conquered those around you
with your openness and charm,
drawn to you, like you were to rock,
centred and solid, resonant
in voice, looks and spirit

and when something slipped inside
it was just the next struggle to win.
when told the chances were slim
you just said you'd booked your ticket

when I first visited, I was terrified to even climb the stairs
but you were sitting up strong
holding our faiths in what you were;
a centre for so many people, through all that pain,
you even stood on the bed, precarious, with no-one's help,
while we watched you, one hand steady on the ceiling,
thread with the other, the origami of bright fragile birds

your whole life, you never took your eyes off the summit
for others as much as yourself; you cajoled your pupils
to pick through doctrines, to find their own routes,
and you led a path through lies, on picket lines,
at work; anywhere you could make a stand

and unspoken in those visits
the way you gripped our hand
or looked up to the mobile
you seemed determined
that we remember
the message
of everything you did:

    climb

Whitby, Jan 2007
for Jenny

we were in our element that day
remembering the evening before
by the ruinous beauty of the abbey
and exposed to the bay, we both felt the thrill
of stormy skies, the blameless promise of open sea
while imagining how boats would struggle
gale whipped
into this gothic harbour
hugged by rugged slopes

Bram Stoker wrote
Dracula here
tagged the town
with his dark romantic imagination
and in the fright museum
we laughed at how scared we were
by 'electronic special effects'
-puppets jerking out on creaky mechanics
and canned horror laughter

but my heart really leapt to my mouth
in the raw January sun
on Whitby beach
when I asked you
to join your blood with mine
      for eternity

Peace is a Park in Sheffield
For Peace in the Park Sheffield community festival

Peace is a Park in Sheffield
Peace is a park full of people
It's a festifull of unconscripted energy
A carnivalesque cornucopian orgy of freedom and fun
Only a heartbeat away from the bullet and the bomb

Peace in the Park will not be televised on Sky
It will not be brought to you by McDonalds,
Coca Cola or British Aerospace:
It will be brought to you by you
By people like you and unlike you

Who all share this
That Peace is a Park in Sheffield
Or at least
A chrysalis becoming butterfly
Of what we want it to be

A Specific Theory of Relativity

not that he didn't venture opinions
rather they were hedged
with a tangle of provisos

nor that he didn't have beliefs
just that they were fashionably flexible
and he'd even express remnants of radicalism
as long as his tongue was tasting his cheek

and when he died one day,
a pastiche of tears *were* expressed
but they were transient, and left no trace:
he might have smiled at that
        wryly

Think the Unthinkable

In the genesis of New Labour, the party was encouraged to 'Think The Unthinkable' (i.e. think like a Tory)

Think the Unthinkable

In my case, witty retaliations have not so much
been just on the tip of my tongue,
but strangled, deep in my throat
or ejaculating premature
yet performing majestically
in retrospective fantasies

like in that ramble through Hathersage, lost,
rumbled by a headscarfed horsey wasp
trying to round the battlements of her country house,
forlorn admissions of incompetence and pleas for sympathy
no match for the scorn of a woman torn from croquet
my bomber jacket no match for her Barbour

ideally, I'd have thought of a more demanding challenge
than 'Are you the Queen?'
made a quip more historically appropriate than
'This isn't prehistoric times you know!'
but probably retained the parting Wildean wit
of "Fuck off you stuck up Tory witch."

my second name was never Dean
and good manners are hard to kick
but alone in a bed, on a bus or a train
we can always get our own back
and dream

and it takes me back, to long before new Labour even thought of it
that my boss at the Co-Op was practising sharp stakeholding
via his line manger, who with her caring female touch

handed me to the High Priest upstairs, a level above
the apples of temptation that I'd display in fruit and veg,
where it transpired that the manager of all these natural delights
had been unbeknown to me, studying my lack of time and motion,
or more arbitrarily, maybe just decided, that I was sacrifice of the week.

I should have turned then on my priestess
not simpered in my seat
"Et tu Brutess?" I could have lamented.
and when treated to a speech from the almighty
about how he got where he was today,
timed as a youth, for how fast he fed the chickens
by a farmer who hid with a stopwatch, behind the coops,

I might politely have suggested,
that if it really had taught him a thing or two
shouldn't it be to be wary of any man
who spies on young boys with farmyard animals
rather than a model for his life plan,
and that I'd rather be dead, than where he was today.

but the best would be, mock naivety;
take any ex-workplace
like the factory floor of British Aerospace
stripping excess metal glue from parts
using a solution that betrayed its power
through fumes through a mask
to a throb in the head

when the foreman brought round a circular
announcing with glee a new multi-million deal
I'd take that rarely trod path up to the offices
knock on the door and kindly ask the bosses

does this mean double pay?
or at least a training day
on new methods of cleaning metal
that stripped only glue
and not brain cells as well?

or for team building
an exercise in exchange
where we work up in the gods
adding zeros to bonuses
and options to share options
while *you* work
on the same section
all your life, cos *we* can't be bothered to move you,
working out the options on a hundred and fifty a week
beer and fags or a holiday out of town
overtime, or free time: *you* choose

or after polishing that missile release unit
one hundred too many times
I'd refuse to continue until I got a guarantee
that it would only be used to kill
really bad people
and maybe suggest a few

and in my restaged life
I'd be gloating, riding high,
jobless, poor,
but with a life you could make a film of,
or a poem

Sealocrete is a cement factory in Shirley, Southampton

"Fuck Off"

The factories are prisons. This is not a metaphor
                                        Foucault

it's difficult to pin down
what was different about Paul
a little more cocky?
a little more scared?
but he was the subject of ethics debates in the tea room;
like is being on probabation for hitting a copper
excuse enough for running from a fight
that he'd started?
and I liked him from my first day
when he asked me for a lift to the police station
he had to sign-on there
and a day of bagging concrete together
was all he needed to ask

not that it was unusual to be on probation or bail
it was more of a requirement of working at Sealocrete, Shirley,

but while the others would tease me and call me 'Brains'
because I was going to university
he seemed to just see me as a workmate, and a help
like when he had to fill in a form
and though the others could mostly read and write
he knew that with me
I wouldn't laugh at his vulnerability
sensing we had at least that in common

because there was something different about Paul
like he'd been humiliated once more
or hit once more, than the rest

so when he would ask me along to drink
at a Shirley pub they'd not been banned from
I felt quite flattered
but scared of not fitting into the Sealocrete pub-fighting team
or of ending up like Dave
off sick one day
from having a chair accidentally wrapped round his head
in friendly-fire
so I made excuses
and just felt guilty
and relieved

like after I'd finished to go to university
and I came in to say goodbye and collect my pay
and I just wanted to walk away
from the warmth with which everyone wished me luck
gathered
standing in the dust

but Paul kept his distance
and I was thrown by this new hostility
he took the piss out of my new shoes
no laughter
and threw an empty sack at them
and then another
as he carried on loading the machine
the one that seemed to take forever
to fill just once
his eyes were fixed on infinity
and he told me to fuck off

International Currency Exchanges

I picked him up coming onto the M1
from Nova Scotia, via Italy
he had to hold the seatbelt off his chest
his ribs cracked from the beating

Fish-farm labourers, he and his brother
at the toss of a coin shared a year's earnings:
hard labour; his brother was to come next year
he was to be the first to slip the net; lucked out

until Milan, when his ride took a twist
down a dead-end, and three desperados
turned on their hitcher, sure
they had him hooked

not knowing how much he had to lose:
a year of sacrifice, in hard cash.
he fought like the marlin
in the Hemmingway yarn

even netted against a fence
with a knife pulled on him.
he showed me the bandaged finger
minus the end they'd de-scaled

and the tip of tooth, one of theirs
taken from his knuckle by a nurse
that he'd kept as some kind of
balance of payment

his Embassy wouldn't lone him a cent.
after a 12 hour hitch he wasted the same time at Calais
foundering on the rock of English hospitality
begging for a ride that'd cost the driver nothing
in exchange for his climbing gear

a Scot landed him in England
and he was now pulsing upstream
to a family source in Ireland

he said that if he went home now
the only legacy of this migration
from his spawning ground
would be to hate all Europeans;
he wouldn't be beaten;
he'd borrow money from home,
carry on regardless

we moved on to work, unions, politics.
in '84 to'85 he and fellow workers gave
to collections his union made
for the miners on our distant shores;
a far-flung net, drawn tight.

the Poll Tax Riot came up,
how he and his brother had watched it on TV
from his small village in Nova Scotia
and cheered from across the ocean
at those who fought the cops back
as they charged us in Trafalgar Square

I left him at a services
with what spare cash I had.
less would have shamed me.
shamed us all

Address to the People on Ending *The Temporary State of Mobilization Against Communist Insurrection*

Note: The poem's title quotes the term used by the Taiwanese government for its constitution, a state formed by the Nationalists who fled China after the revolution. Chiang Kai-shek led the Kuomintang who ruled Taiwan at the time of this poem's writing-1991. He was superseded by his son Chiang Ching-kuo. 'Mainland memories' refers to Nationalist massacres of thousands involved in pre-Revolution workers' uprisings in China.

in the concrete shadow of Chiang Kai-shek
in service to ancestral ghosts
the old woman, the new woman
    burning at this shrine
sanctified notes of no value at all
echo
in the hired chambers of my heart
the impotent prayers, and sterilized votes
that whirl in a furnace which only inflames
    an opening phoenix

in the concrete shadow of Chiang Ching-kuo
illusions going up in smoke
and coming back down
              in careless chemical waste
    the boss's cock-sure smile
    and that accidental body screaming in the street
who no one will touch for fear of being sued

but through the holy complacency
that stains these spat-out streets
with the bitterness of areca blood
    I have been embraced by children
and I catch your eye and desire
to reach in and drag out your heart

        into open air
selfishly
knowing it would last no longer
than a butterfly in the spirit-money smog of this city
shadowed by the slow circling of your latest Premier
and is he a Taoist, is he a Christian, is he a Native?
I'm a vulture, I'm a vulture, what kind of vulture am I?

for even in the mountains
which have no time for the ghost of Chiang Kai-shek
whose statues stalk the ruined cities, their uniform stiff
with the slow blood of mainland memories
a multitude of heroes from an age of dreams
worth more than its weight in dollars, with which he is plastered
and even beyond the final retreats of hill tribes
in places unsold   and hushed in mist
there is a dust in the air more insidious
than the arbitrary by-products of industry
that resigns the demobilized excursionists
to knowledge of why the air weeps from every pore
and that until the worship ends
this land will know more sadness than the rain
that baptizes these bamboo hills
again and again
with a tainted legacy

Coping with Maggots

diesel engines rumble
idling ominously in the yard
on the steps to the office
class conflict
crystalised to four letter words
then to something harder and sharper:
the trucks wouldn't move till this was sorted

to them we were *city hygiene operatives*
to us we were bin-men
chugging through the dawn streets
in cabs blind with fag-smoke
thrown off the footplate gasping
impacting on tarmac with shocked knees

we'd run the whole round to free up time
for overtime, jogging up side alleys and returning
with more than our backs could take
the oldest men's shape broken under the weight of waste
the youngest bodies still rising to the strain
hard as fuck, but soft as love

they joked that students never lasted
but from the start carried my weight
split the scam money in equal parts
once tried to give me a big bag of chops;
bosses break the rules for yachts and sports cars
for us it was a free chip buttie and a cuppa
or a pint at the end of the round.

I had no taste for chops, but never forgot
the taste of the comradeship of the cab and the streets
an antidote to the tabloid trash of tits and arse
bigotry and bullying, chewed and belched out
in the canteen, and the strip pubs

kindness quenched our thirsty sinews;
a glass left by a tap glistened on a scorching day
when we stripped to the waist, sunned and sweating
or tea in someone's kitchen
steaming away the groggy cold window of morning

we weren't that pleased with the maggots bred in bins
they'd end up on your overalls
from the bags you'd fling on your back
but what was bred in management stunk worse
like not showing me the safety video
so when I chucked that fridge in the crusher
I didn't look away, and nearly lost my eyes, stung by fluid
rushing half-blind to someone's bathroom sink.
on our streets the doors were always open

that day, Rob's baby was due, wife on the edge of labour
dependent on his, but needing him there,
all he wanted from them was the afternoon off;
overtime anyway, and a gesture of humanity.
they prioritised
and directed Rob to work an extra shift and miss his baby's birth

hydraulics hissed
pent up pressure put to piston
and the hulking great back-jawed beasts
circled the yard
the trucks wouldn't move till this was sorted
the bin-men's muscle put to use
and the maggots
crushed

Epitaphs for Larkin

After his ditty from *Letters:*

> *I'd like to see them starving*
> *The so-called working-class*
> *Their wages yearly halving*
> *Their women eating grass*

1 **'All that will survive of us is love'**

I'd like to see him awaken
To a victorious working-class
Grasp the life for which they'd striven
And his heart break open like glass

2 **Nobbled Laureates**

I'd like to see them working
The so-called ruling class
And no more money going
To poets who kiss their arse

1. The first title is a quote from one of his poems.
2. Larkin was never Laureate, but I doubt he'd have written this.

The Emperor's New Socialism

As the Emperor paraded
while his Empire crumbled
a small child pointed
to the businessmen at his table
and the workers at his feet
and she laughed until she cried

Paper Chase

On your Marx

in the 'race to the bottom'
for competitive wages
the faster you run
the more you lose.
except for the man with the starter gun
behind you
loaded

Get debt

born into debt
the African child
is still a slave
to the paper-thin counterfeit power
of a pale queen or president's head
enthroned on the new body-politic
of Global Capital

Go

In Barcelona
the World Bank
like Franco before
are driven out by a deeper rooted power
and the trees on La Ramblas
shed blossom in remembrance

Notes:
May 2001: World Bank Barcelona meeting cancelled due to fear of anti-capitalist protest.
In Barcelona: in the 1930s Civil War, Barcelona was for a while under democratic workers' control and a stronghold of resistance to Franco's Fascists (brilliantly captured in Orwell's *Homage to Catalonia*).

Rumble in the Jungle

when Ali fought Foreman
Zaire was still the Congo
to many
but it was clearly black
when he put it on the map
for America to see
like when he refused the draft for Vietnam
'cos no Vietnamese never called me nigger'
and the dispossessed of Kinshasa and Harlem
flooded the streets with
chants for Ali
Even though Foreman had the weight
and the piston-punch
of a man used to victory

and when, after holding back
and taking it
for round
after round
after round
When that lightning right
came out of hiding
in a flurry of focused revenge
and Ali raised his fists in victory

the heavyweights of society
the world over
hesitated
and those who'd taken the beating for years
sang in the streets

Smoulder and Spark

Red Carpet

Bush and Blair hold court for the press
and extend their crippled consciences
to autocue condolences
for casualties owned as 'ours'

and although they leave
the Iraqi dead and maimed
unmentioned

if you listen
behind their moving lips
there is a sound of murder
murmering at first
but growing to a thunder

and if you look
beneath their feet
there is blood rolling out
like a red carpet
into all our futures

During the war on Afghanistan in 2001, politicians made play of dropping token amounts of food, in between bombing raids.

Dropping Bombs and Food

yeah they're dropping bombs and food
for freedom and democracy
they're dropping bombs and food

they say they want to liberate you
cos suddenly they care
but they'll bury you under rubble
and their voters under lies
of guided footage
dead on target
via TV eyes

yeah they're dropping bombs and food
for freedom and democracy
they're dropping bombs and food

and you can trek by the million
to relentless borders
but you'd better watch your step
because they've sown your soil
with cluster bombs
a harvest bright for children's eyes

yeah they're dropping bombs and food
for freedom and democracy
they're dropping bombs and food

they'll select your opposition
a puppet show from hell
and tell you to be grateful
for a bombed out ghostly shell

yeah they're dropping bombs and food
for freedom and democracy
they're dropping bombs
                          and bombs
        and bombs
                          and bombs

and food

This has been produced as a song, by a punk band called The Ropey Shags which you may have heard, though you'd have to be into German punk, in fact, German punk from the town of Wuppertal.

March 2000: The Blairs visit Russian President Putin, to cement approval for his role as a 'Westerniser'. They are also met by the head of the World Bank, Wolfensohn. All are responsible for pushing the free-market capitalism which devastated the Russian economy and ordinary people's standard of living. Putin was Chief of the KGB, now called the FSB, whose agents were caught red-handed planting explosives in a Moscow block of flats. Previous explosions had been blamed on Chechen terrorists, and used to justify the Russian war against Chechnya

War and Peace: Stage Management
'Our countries are natural partners' - Downing Street

appreciating the finer things in life
should come naturally to Tony and Vladimir
Cherie and Lyudmila
as they engage in Czarist footsteps
at the summer palace, Petrodvorets
whilst Chechen children dance to their tune
guessing which footfall will clear a mine

and over caviar and champagne at the Kirov
as the Blairs toast with Wolfensohn
to the 'westerniser' Putin
will the unpaid and unemployed of Russia
raise vodka to their broken lips
to praise this 'successful and engaged nation'?

and up in the gods, as the curtain rises on *War and Peace*
will glasses be clinked together
as Grozny windows shatter?

and what kind of smile will the ex-KGB lieutenant smile
as Downing Street recycles excuses
whose familiarity lingers Orange on their lips:
'there is a terrorist insurrection on their territory'
and the FSB plant hatred for Chechens
in working-class Moscow flats.

        in the theatre
the curtain falls
             and the audience applause
     explodes

and far off
     apartment blocks of lives
                 collapse in silence

The quotes in speech-marks are from newspaper reports of a meeting between Bush and Blair, between the attacks on Afghanistan and Iraq.

The Hidden Fist

'The hidden hand of the market will never work without the hidden fist. McDonalds cannot flourish without McDonnell Douglas'
                                        Right-wing US commentator

'All smiles as Blair and Bush meet'
and faced the world's press:

the hidden fist

'a pretty charming guy':

the hidden fist

'there'll always be a friend on the other end of the
   phone':

the hidden fist

Afghanistan
Fourteen
burying his mother
desert wind
relentless sun
like a million camera flashes silent:

the hidden fist

This was written after watching news coverage of NATO bombing of Belgrade early in the war on Serbia, whilst I was at a Trade Union conference in Brighton.

Satellite Links

Satellite news transmits searing
flames to my hotel room, delivers
the shell-shocked rescued babies
removed from the ward next to the target

And I watch impotently
As once again we bomb
Justice into an ungrateful populous
I leave the hotel, needing air

There's something World War Two about Brighton tonight
tawdry amusements and Bank Holiday crowds,
union jacks tug impatiently in the dark,
storm clouds.

I drift down to the night beach
to breath in a disturbed sea and pall gray sky;
the pier pierces this backdrop,
a fluorescent strip of fairground lights

unreal
ablaze
distant echoes of screaming

Smoulder and Spark
February 15th 2003

an inferno of people
we move like wildfire
a million or two,
enough,
to set this capital ablaze
with a call to peace,
one flow, of a driving molten core
that falters for no borders
and blossoms today
in continent after continent
country after country
city after city
roaring through the streets
with the same flame

so that others may not burn
in villages and cities
wrapped calmly
in napalm and uranium
whilst we become frozen
in the dark ice of war
in lies and complicity

night descends, winged
with the bitterness of winter
of a government's veins
clogged with oil

near Speakers' Corner
waiting for coaches and resisting the cold
a group of protestors build a fire
sustainable and protective,
made for instance,
of no-one's home,
and we feed the flames
of something good

under-orders
pistol-like
the police move in
stamp the fire
stir up sparks
restore cold
move us out
lock the gate
return the park
to its keepers:
to silence and security

but the scattered embers
still smoulder and spark
bright against the gathering dark

Taste and Decency

British troops shown on TV
when dead
offend the sense of taste and decency
of the commander who sent them to die

well-
missiles in marketplaces
uranium stillbirths
billion dollar budgets
for death and destruction
a roadmap for Israel
with bulldozers and tanks
thrown in for free
ruling class leaders
of working class sacrifice
anti-war protesters
arrested and charged
for breach of the peace
riot police on our streets
and state terrorists
in our houses of parliament:

these things
offend our sense
of taste and decency

when we could have-

food in all the marketplaces
and billion dollar budgets
for health and reconstruction
a roadmap for Palestine
drawn by Palestinians
working class leaders
of ruling class sacrifice
riot police off our streets,
anti-war protesters

in our houses of parliament
and state terrorists
arrested and charged
for breach of the peace:

these things
would start to satisfy
our sense
of taste and decency

Sculpture Poems

To Carl Danby:
Thanks so much for sharing this project

These were written to accompany sculptures by Carl Danby.

Yin Yang

the jaws of unity
ache to close
the tongue is thick
with only fear

Worter Macht Frei

Notes: The entrance to Auscwitz says *Arbeit Macht Frei* (Work makes you free). *Worter* means words. Marek Edelman's first-hand account of the Warsaw Ghetto uprising, *The Ghetto Fights*, is compelling reading).

The Book
Steel and Paper
C Danby   1994

>Compressed in the Ghetto walls of Warsaw
>Only the cattle trucks led you out.
>The last few thousand chose another way,
>and answered The Song of The Partisan:
>*If not this way, how?*
>*If not now, when?*
>Starved, isolated, poorly armed
>you were the Nazi's Vietcong;
>repelling wave after wave of SS attacks
>until to save their military honour
>they burnt you out with firestorms
>like those that awaited you
>in an even darker place
>
>Few of you survived

but your legend escaped that furnace
floating like ashes
a phoenix of words
that ignited history
a legend partisans carried across Europe like a flame
to feed the final fight

Epilogue: Fahrenheit 451

Fahrenheit 451 is the temperature book-paper ignites, and is the title of Ray Bradbury's dystopian novel, set in a future where books are burnt.

Amnesia and cowardice
Are the temperature truth burns at
We who face no death squads
Face ourselves

Spirals

These sculptures are like giant wind-chimes, made of glass, filled with water, which can be walked through

I

Water, glass and air spiral
And we thirst
For our wild, unattainable
Dreams of purity

II

We navigate through
Our desires, terrified
That if touched
We'd make them sing

III

We navigate through
Our dreams, afraid
That if touched
They'd shatter

Untitled

Our bodies sing
The bright and
Distant glory
Of our warm
Dark blood

Kashmir

Kashmir
For Abdul Assim

this ancient glacial gorge
swings an epic swathe
through sheer velvet hills
sweeping through millennia
like the Moguls and British who followed
fierce and unrelenting
carving deep, embedded division

but as an earthquake's insurrection
can reshape these mountains
so these people will find a way
to shake themselves free

Dust to Dust

delivered from detachment
right into the thick it
on the back of a motorbike
swept up in a swirl of dust, shalwaar-kameez, bare feet, cheerful shouting,
I'm deep in play before I get the chance to feel out of my depth-
rushing through tufts of waste-ground grass
the way football was first played- free, anarchic, democratic-
at least three games interweaving, and at one point
I'm all at sea, following the wrong ball
the next free kick I'm offered first
and when I scuff it way off target
they insist it was a great shot,
I'm told to play up front
given the best balls
never tackled hard
and in between bouts of play I'm salaamed
and complimented on my few words of amateur urdu
asked my opinion on their people and on politics

and I wonder
as we mingle in the dust
as dusk approaches
if I come back in a year or two
as all around us war encroaches
will we be able
to play like this
again

For my Comrades in Bagh

as the weeks unfold
the fullness of these people
is unveiled
and the label muslim peels away
to reveal them more clearly

like in that cafe in Bagh
suspended in the hills of Azad Kashmir
when I shared tea and ideas
with the friends and trotskyists
of Kashmir Class Struggle
bonding in their belief
that we're better connected
by struggle
than by aid

and walking home later
the army sentry
sullen at the his post
in the burgeoning twilight
a colonial legacy
of divide and rule
still clutched a rifle
but seemed to us then
a lot less permanent

Untitled, Bagh 2006

mist pours down
these lush tortured hills
and the gorge is filled with snaking water
rushing toward a distant sea

and I could say the rain here falls
like tears, but this town already
is flooded with its own

enough even
to fill these swollen rivers
for the thousands lost under rubble and mud
and the rain that drums all night
on canvas and corrugated metal
could never drown out the ghosts
the trapped cries they still hear

Mumna cradles her sister's baby
looks at me sadly
and says 'she cries for her mother'

and I wish I could say
that this rain will wash away their tears
to join the water in the valley
rushing toward a distant sea

Epilogue

Escapology

You fix the trainer with untamed eyes
And find a rhythm that threads the ring
With muscled grace of shimmering thighs
Hear every cell in your body sing
This circus god your jaws can frame
So make them sweat and keep them wary
Today is unwrit and may not be the same
As the past or prophesied neat finale
The bars are taunting your angry sighs
Look raw at those who sponsor your fate
Unlock the fierceness of your eyes
To pace the steps to the open gate;
Ask what commandment or plea
Can frame thy fearful energy…

And reply

Any comments you have would be much appreciated. Let me know at 1jamesoliver@gmail.com